1001 Kids' JOKES

1001 Kids' JOKES

KAY BARNHAM

Sandy Creek
NEW YORK

Sandy Creek
NEW YORK

An Imprint of Sterling Publishing
387 Park Avenue South
New York, NY 10016

ISBN 978-1-4351-5310-3

Author: Kay Barnham
Editor: Kate Overy

Design and Illustration by *Q* CREATIVE QUOTIENT

Manufactured in Malaysia
Lot #:
2 4 6 8 10 9 7 5 3 1
01/14

CONTENTS

Get ready to giggle yourself silly!

Are you ready to laugh so hysterically that it feels worse than being tickled? Are you ready for 1001 side-splitting sniggers? If you like laughter more than a jelly likes to wobble, then read on!

1001 Kids' Jokes is jam-packed full of the funniest, silliest, craziest jokes around and there's something for everyone! From knock, knock jokes to classic chuckles, you'll have your friends and family in stitches for hours… days… years! In fact, if you tell enough of these gags, you'll probably be known as the funniest person in the world.

So, take a deep breath and prepare for 1001 of the most eye-wateringly funny jokes ever!

AMUSING ANIMALS

A grizzly bear walked into a café and said,
"I'll have a glass of milk … and a brownie."
The waitress looked at him and said, "What's with the big paws?"

❖

Did you hear about the cat who sucked a lemon?
He was a sourpuss.

❖

Why don't elephants like playing cards in the jungle?
Because of all the cheetahs.

❖

Did you hear about the crocodile with the camera?
He was snap-happy.

Did you hear about the duck who went to the comedy show?
He quacked up.

How did the puppy stop the DVD?
He used paws.

How do chicks get out of their shells?
They eggs-it.

How do you get down from a camel?
You don't. You get down from a goose.

What do alligators call little children?
Appetizers.

What's a pig's favorite ballet?
Swine Lake.

My dog's a blacksmith.

How can you tell?

When I tell him off, he makes a bolt for the door.

What does a cat do when it gets angry?

It goes up the wall.

Why did the pony cough?

Because he was a little hoarse.

What did the duck say when she bought lipstick?

"Put it on my bill."

One boy says to another boy, "My pet's called Tiny."

"Why?" asks his friend.

"Because he's my newt."

There are two birds sitting on a perch.

What does one bird say to the other bird?

"Smells of fish."

How do you stop a rhinoceros from charging?
Take away its credit cards.

What did the chicken say when it laid a square egg?
Owwww!

What did the frog order at the burger bar?
Some French flies and a Diet Croak.

What sort of music do rabbits like best?
Hip-hop.

Why are bats never lonely?
They always hang around with their friends.

❖

What do cats like to watch on television?
The evening mews.

❖

Why was the firefly mother disappointed?
Because her children weren't very bright.

❖

Why did the farmer buy a brown cow?
He wanted to get chocolate milk.

❖

What do cats eat for breakfast?
Mice Krispies.

❖

What do sheep do when the weather's hot?
Have a baa-baa-cue.

What do killer whales eat for dinner?
Fish and ships.

❖

What side of a porcupine is the sharpest?
The outside.

❖

What do you call a homeless snail?
A slug.

❖

Why do giraffes have such long necks?
Because they have very smelly feet.

What do you call a cat who swallows a duck?
A duck-filled fatty-puss.

What did the grape say when the elephant stepped on him?
Nothing. He just let out a little wine.

What do you call a sleeping bull?
A bulldozer.

❖

Where does the biggest spider ever live?
On the world wide web.

What do you get if you cross a frog with a small dog?
A croaker spaniel.

❖

What do you get if you cross an elephant with a mouse?
Huge holes in the baseboard.

❖

Why do fish live in salt water?
Because pepper makes them sneeze.

❖

Why do elephants never forget?
Because no one ever tells them anything.

❖

What do you get if you cross a computer with an elephant?
Loads of memory.

❖

What did one flea say to the other before going out?
Shall we walk or take the dog?

What happens when two snails have a fight?
They slug it out.

What do you give a pig with sore muscles?
Oinkment.

What flies through the jungle singing opera?
The Parrots of Penzance.

What happened when the sheep's pen broke?
The sheep had to use a pencil.

What did the buffalo say when he dropped his boy at school?
Bison.

What goes black-white-black-white-black-white?
A penguin rolling down a hill.

What do you get if you cross a kangaroo and an elephant?
Very big holes in your lawn.

What goes "oo oo"?
A cow with no lips.

What happened to the cat who swallowed a ball of wool?
She had mittens.

What do you get from a nervous cow?
Milkshakes.

What do you call a fly with no wings?
A walk.

What is a cat's favorite color?
Purrple.

❖

Why do pet shops always sell out of birds before any other animal?
Because they go cheep.

❖

What is a cat's favorite party game?
Mewsical chairs.

What do dogs eat at the movies?
Pupcorn.

❖

What did the fish say when he swam into a wall?
Dam!

❖

What do you call cows that are lying down?
Ground beef.

❖

Why is there no point playing jokes on snakes?
You can't pull their legs.

❖

Which dogs love to have their hair washed?
Shampoodles.

❖

What name did the snail give to his home?
Michelle.

What should you never do with an angry rhinoceros?
Argue.

What time is it when an elephant sits on your bike?
Time to get a new bike.

What type of cows eat grass?
Lawn moo-ers.

What's a snake's favorite subject?
Hisssstory.

Why do leopards make terrible thieves?
They are always spotted.

What did one sheep say to the other sheep?
"After ewe."

What goes 99-thump-99-thump-99-thump?
A centipede with a wooden leg.

What noise does an exploding monkey make?
BaBOON!!!

What party game do cows like best?
Moosical chairs.

❖

What should you do if you find a gorilla sleeping in your bed?
Sleep somewhere else!

What's an elephant's favorite game?
Squash.

What has a hundred legs and can see just as well from both ends?
A centipede with its eyes shut.

What's green, cold-blooded, and follows the yellow brick road?
The Lizard of Oz.

What goes "oom oom"?
A cow walking backward.

When does a horse give a straight answer?
Whinny wants to.

❖

What do you get if you cross a dinosaur with a tea party?
A tyrannosaucer.

❖

What's the difference between a fly and a bird?
A bird can fly, but a fly can't bird.

❖

Why is a swordfish's nose 11 inches long?
If it were 12 inches long, it would be a foot.

❖

What do you call a dinosaur with a cowboy hat?
Tyrannosaurus Tex.

❖

What's the last thing that goes through a fly's mind
as it hits the car windshield?
Its bottom.

What did the pig say when the farmer grabbed him by the tail?
"That's the end of me."

What does a cat rest its head on at night?
A caterpillow.

What kind of insect can't make up its mind?
A maybe.

What's worse than raining cats and dogs?
Hailing taxis.

When can three elephants get under an umbrella
and not get wet?
When it isn't raining.

❖

Where do insects do their shopping?
At a flea market.

❖

Where do sharks come from?
Finland.

❖

What type of bone will a dog never eat?
A trombone.

❖

Where do you find an upside-down tortoise?
Where you left it.

❖

How did the frog feel after she broke her leg?
Unhoppy.

Where does a monkey cook burgers?
Under a gorilla.

❖

Which animal do you find on a legal document?
A seal.

❖

Which animal was out of bounds?
The exhausted kangaroo.

❖

Which bird always sounds out of breath?
A puffin.

❖

Which insect works on a construction site?
A crane fly.

❖

What do you call two birds who have fallen in love?
Tweethearts.

What animal loves a good novel?
A bookworm.

What's gray, has four legs, and a trunk?
A mouse going on vacation.

Which reptile would you find relaxing on the sofa?
A lounge lizard.

What do caterpillars do on New Year's Day?
Turn over a new leaf.

What's the healthiest type of insect?
The vitamin bee.

Why are dogs such bad dancers?
They have two left feet.

What do you call a cow with no milk?
An udder failure.

❖

Why couldn't the elephant twins go swimming at the pool?
Because they only had one pair of trunks between them.

Why did the sparrow use a pair of tongs on her tail feathers?
She thought it was the curly bird who gets the worm.

❖

Why did the lion spit out the clown?
Because he tasted funny.

❖

Why did the tiny terrier puppy bite people's ankles?
He couldn't reach any higher.

❖

Why didn't the shrimp like to share?
Because it was a little shellfish.

❖

Why do birds fly south in the winter?
Because it's too far to walk.

❖

Why do bees have sticky hair?
Because they use honeycombs.

Why do gorillas have big nostrils?
Because they have big fingers!

Why do mice need oiling?
Because they squeak.

What do frogs wear on their feet in the summer?
Open-toad sandals.

Why do lions eat raw meat?
Because they don't know how to use ovens.

Where do rabbits go after they're married?
On bunnymoon.

Why do toadstools grow so closely together?
Because they don't need mushroom.

Why were the geese overweight?
They couldn't stop gobbling.

When do squirrels say, "woof woof"?
When they eat acorns and bark.

How can you tell that carrots help you see in the dark?
Have you ever seen a rabbit with a lantern?

What weighs a lot and wears glass slippers?
Cinderellephant.

What do mice do when they get a new home?
They throw a mouse warming party!

A policeman saw a man walking down the street with a penguin. He told the man to take the penguin to the zoo.

"Good idea," the man said, and off he went.

The next day, the policeman saw the man again. He still had the penguin with him.

"I told you to take that penguin to the zoo," the policeman said.

"I did," the man replied. "He really enjoyed that, so today I'm taking him to the movies."

THE LAUGHTER LIBRARY

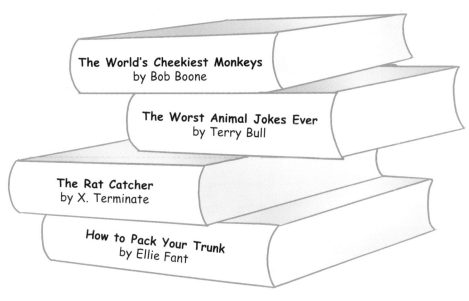

The World's Cheekiest Monkeys
by Bob Boone

The Worst Animal Jokes Ever
by Terry Bull

The Rat Catcher
by X. Terminate

How to Pack Your Trunk
by Ellie Fant

CLASSIC CHUCKLES

Why did the chicken cross the road?
To get to the other side.

Why did the pterodactyl cross the road?
Because chickens didn't exist then.

What did the farmer use to repair his shirt?
A cabbage patch.

Why did Captain Hook cross the road?
To get to the second hand shop.

Why did the chicken cross the playground?
To get to the other slide.

Why did the chicken cross the road, jump in a muddy ditch,
and cross back over the road again?
Because he was a dirty double-crosser.

How many chickens does it take to change a lightbulb?
None, they're all too busy crossing the road.

A girl walks into a shop and says, "I'd like to buy a wasp, please."
"But we don't sell any wasps," says the owner.
"That's funny," says the girl. "You have one in your window."

How can you keep a wet dog from smelling?
Hold its nose.

How many babysitters does it take to change a lightbulb?
None. Lightbulbs don't wear diapers.

How many crime writers does it take to change a lightbulb?
**Two. One to screw it in and the other to
give it a good twist at the end.**

How many police officers does it take to screw in a lightbulb?
None. It turned itself in.

How many cashiers does it take to change a lightbulb?
One, as long as you have the receipt.

Knock knock.
Who's there?
Cash.
Cash who?
No, thanks. I prefer walnuts.

Knock knock.
Who's there?
The interrupting cow.
The interrupting cow wh—
MOOOOOOOOOOO!

What's red and black and red and black?
A zebra with a sunburn.

Knock knock.

Who's there?

Police.

Police who?

Police let us in. It's freezing out here!

What's black and white and noisy?

A zebra with a drum machine.

What's black and white and red all over?

A newspaper.

Knock knock.

Who's there?

Arthur.

Arthur who?

Arthur any cookies left?

Knock knock.

Who's there?

Scott.

Scott who?

Scott nothing to do with you!

Knock knock.

Who's there?

Little old lady.

Little old lady who?

I didn't know you could yodel!

What's black and white and black and white and green?
Two zebras fighting over a pickle.

Why did the man run around his bed each night?
He was trying to catch up on his sleep.

Knock knock.

Who's there?

Snow.

Snow who?

Snow business like show business.

❖

Knock knock.

Who's there?

Doughnut.

Doughnut who?

Doughnut open until your birthday!

❖

What gets wetter the more it dries?

A towel.

❖

What's black and white and eats like a horse?

A zebra.

What do you call a man with a car on his head?

Jack.

Knock knock.

Who's there?

Doris.

Doris who?

Doris locked. That's why I had to knock!

Knock knock.

Who's there?

Tank.

Tank who?

You're welcome!

What begins with "e" and ends with "e" and has a letter in the middle?

An envelope.

Knock knock.

Who's there?

Boo.

Boo who?

Don't cry. It's only a joke.

Knock knock.

Who's there?

Hawaii.

Hawaii who?

I'm fine, thanks. How are you?

Knock knock.

Who's there?

Archie.

Archie who?

Bless you!

Why did the chicken cross the basketball court?

Because the referee whistled for a fowl.

Knock knock.

Who's there?

Ya.

Ya who?

What are you getting so excited about?

Why did the orange stop in
the middle of the road?
Because he ran out of juice.

Why should you never trust atoms?
Because they make everything up.

Which nails do carpenters hate hammering?
Fingernails!

What does a clock do when it's hungry?
Goes back four seconds.

Did you hear about the magical tractor?
It turned into a field.

What do you call a man with a seagull on his head?

Cliff.

Knock knock.
Who's there?
A lass.
A lass who?
Isn't that what cowboys use?

How can you tell if there's an elephant in the fridge?
The door won't shut.

What do you call a man with a trowel in his head?
Doug.

Knock knock.
Who's there?
Candy.
Candy who?
Candy cow jump over the moon?

Knock knock.
Who's there?
Ammonia.
Ammonia who?
Ammonia person collecting for charity!

What do you call a man without a trowel in his head?
Douglas.

What do you call an overeducated plumber?
A drain surgeon.

What should you do if you're attacked by a circus?
Go for the juggler.

Knock knock.
Who's there?
Wanda.
Wanda who?
Wanda wish you a happy birthday!

What do you call a woman who catches lots of fish in one try?
Annette.

Knock knock.
Who's there?
Theresa.
Theresa who?
Theresa green in summer.

Knock, knock.
Who's there?
Dishes.
Dishes who?
Dishes a terrible joke!

What do you call a man with sports equipment on his head?
Jim.

What did the sheet say to the mattress?
"Don't worry—I've got you covered."

❖

What do you call a deer with no eyes?
No idea.

❖

What do you call a deer with no eyes who's totally motionless?
Still no idea.

❖

What did the judge tell the messy witnesses to wear?
Lawsuits.

❖

What do you call a man who stands in front of pop stars?
Mike.

❖

What do you call a lady who thinks only about herself?
Mimi.

Knock knock.
Who's there?
Norma Lee.
Norma Lee who?
Norma Lee I'd ring the doorbell.

Did you hear about the woman who got the
job as the human cannonball?
She was fired.

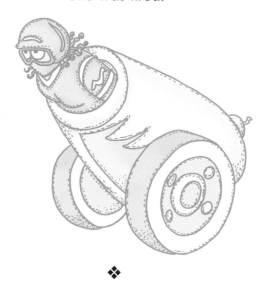

What do you call a giraffe with one leg?
Eileen.

❖

What do you call a man who floats on the sea?
Bob.

What did one angel say to the other angel?
Halo there!

❖

What do you call a man with his pockets stuffed full of paper bags?
Russell.

❖

What do you call a man with rabbits in his pants?
Warren.

❖

What do you call a man who can't stand up?
Neil.

What do you call a woman with a frog on her head?
Lily.

What do you call a camel with three humps?
Humphrey.

When is a door not a door?
When it's ajar.

What's green and goes camping?
A Brussels scout.

Why do elephants paint their toenails red?
So they can hide in strawberry patches.

Why did the two friends choose to study History?
They liked to chat about old times.

What should you feed an elf who wants to be taller?
Elf-rising flour.

On which side of the house did Jack's beanstalk grow?
The outside.

What is an archaeologist?
Someone whose career is in ruins.

Did you hear about the accountant with a stuffed nose?
He worked it out with a pencil.

Why did the code-breaker spend so long in the
percussion section of the orchestra?
He was looking for cymbals.

What happens if a frog parks illegally?
It gets toad.

Why did the jewel thief have a nice, foamy bubble bath before robbing a rich woman?
He wanted to make a clean getaway.

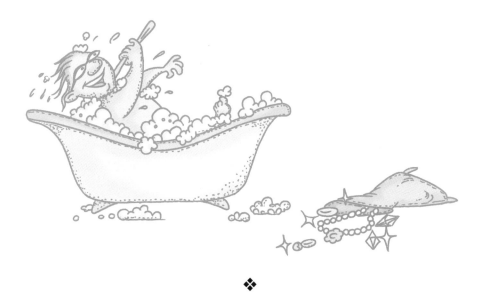

Did you hear about the dizzy boy scout?
He spent all week doing good turns.

Did you hear about the jewel thief who opened a shop?
He used a crowbar.

Did you hear about the man who went
to sleep under the leaky, old car?
He wanted to wake up oily in the morning.

51

Did you hear about the prisoner who talked v-e-r-y slowly?
It took him 15 years to finish his sentence.

Who can shave six times a day and still have a beard?
A barber.

Why are management meetings always so horribly dull?
They're held in the Bored Room.

What do you call a sheep with no legs?
A cloud.

What did the frog say as it washed its window?
"Rub it, rub it, rub it."

❖

What do you call a tree with a croaky voice?
A hoarse chestnut.

❖

Did you hear about the woman with the big fluffy hat called Cynthia?
That's a funny name for a hat.

❖

Have you heard the joke about the bed?
Sorry, it hasn't been made up yet.

❖

Where do pianists go on vacation?
The Florida Keys.

❖

How do you keep a total idiot in suspense?
I'll tell you later.

What type of trees do fortune tellers like?
Palm trees.

What did the firefighter's wife get for Christmas?
A ladder in her stocking.

Why did the girl throw the clock out of the window?
She wanted to see time fly.

What do you get if you drop a grand piano down an elevator shaft?
A flat miner.

What did the highwayman say to the tap-dancing mailman?
Stand and deliver.

How do you know when a filthy robber has taken a bath?
When you can't find it in your bathroom.

What do you get when you cross a dog with an elephant?
A really nervous mailman.

What type of dog can tell the time?
A watchdog.

What happened to the clock that fell into the sheep medicine?
It lost all its ticks.

What did one escalator say to the other escalator?
I think I'm coming down with something.

If you found money in every pocket of your pants,
what would you have?
Someone else's pants.

What do you call a country where everyone has to drive red cars?
A red carnation.

Why wouldn't the bald man lend anyone his comb?
He just couldn't part with it.

How do you make your own antifreeze?
Send her to the Antarctic.

How does a policeman listen to music on the beat?
On his iPlod.

❖

How does Jack Frost travel?
By icicle.

❖

Why did the man bash the giggling fortune teller?
He was striking a happy medium.

❖

What did the scarf say to the hat?
You go on ahead and I'll just hang around.

❖

Why was the clock feeling sick?
It was run down.

❖

Who delivers presents to dogs on Christmas Eve?
Santa Paws.

❖

What's hairy and sneezes?
A coconut with a cold.

What do you get if you dip convicts into quick-drying cement?
Hardened criminals.

Why did the man put his money in the freezer?
He wanted cold, hard cash.

What did one lightbulb say to the other lightbulb?
I'm going out tonight.

What has one foot and four legs?
A bed.

THE LAUGHTER LIBRARY

I Fell Down a Rabbit Hole
by Alyson Wonderland

Over the Cliff
by Hugo First

Classic Fiction
by Warren Peace

When the Wind Blows
by Russell Ingleaves

FUNNY FOOD

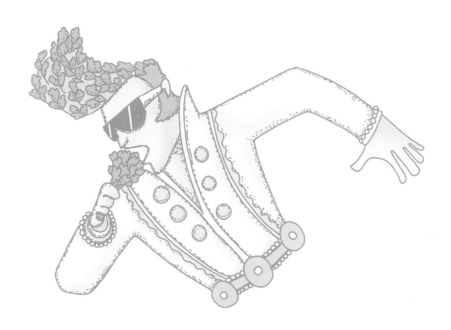

Which type of fruit has the nastiest temper?
A crab apple.

Why did the jelly wobble?
Because it saw the milk shake.

Why didn't the boy with a sausage up his nose and
a chocolate bar in his ear feel well?
He wasn't eating properly.

What's worse than biting into an apple and finding a worm?
Finding half a worm.

What are twins' favorite fruit?

Pears.

What does a pelican order at a restaurant?

Anything that fits the bill.

Have you heard the joke about the butter?

Sorry, I can't tell you because you might spread it.

How do you make a chicken stew?

Keep it waiting for a couple of hours.

What happens if you eat Christmas decorations?

You get tinselitis.

What's the best day of the week to eat ice cream?

Sundae!

How do you make a Mexican chilli?
Send him to Siberia.

How do you make a sausage roll?
Push it down a hill.

Why did the baker stop making doughnuts?
He got sick of the hole business.

What's orange and points North?
A magnetic carrot.

What did the egg in the monastery say?
"Out of the frying pan, into the friar!"

What did the speedy tomato say to the slow tomato?
Ketchup!

What do snowmen eat for breakfast?
Snowflakes.

❖

What color is a burp?
Burple.

❖

How do you make a glass of milkshake?
Give it a fright.

❖

What do you give a dog with a temperature?
**Mustard, relish, and ketchup. They're the
best things for a hot dog.**

How did the banana know he was ill?
He wasn't peeling well.

What did the waiter say when the horse walked into the café?
"Why the long face?"

What do you call a piece of fruit wearing a gag?
Peachless.

What did the baby corn say to the mama corn?
Where's the pop corn?

What do you call a peanut in a spacesuit?
An astronut.

What do you get if you cross a comedian and an orange?
Peels of laughter.

What do you get if you cross a biscuit and a steamroller?
Crumbs.

What did the hamburger parents name their baby daughter?
Patty.

Why did the ant run across the top of the cereal packet?
Because it said, "Tear along the dotted line."

What's orange and doesn't belong to you?
Nacho cheese.

What's the best thing to put in an apple pie?
A spoon.

What did one plate say to the other plate?
Lunch is on me.

What's small, green, round, and goes up, down, up, down?
A pea in an elevator.

Why do the French eat snails?
Because they don't like fast food.

Did you hear about the egg that was tickled too much?
It cracked up.

How do you turn light chocolate into dark chocolate?
Turn the light off.

What do you call a worried turnip?
An edgy veggie.

What starts with T, ends with T, and is full of T?
A teapot.

What is white, has a horn, and gives milk?
A dairy truck.

How do you make a fruit punch?
Give it boxing lessons.

Which part of the sponge cake did the dentist like best?
The filling.

Why did the biscuit cry?
Because his mom had been a wafer so long.

Why did the man eat yeast and furniture polish for breakfast?
He wanted to rise and shine.

What's green, hairy, and goes up, down, up, down?
A kiwifruit on a trampoline.

Why did the management consultant spit food at his client?
He was giving feedback.

Why did the rhubarb go out with a prune?
Because he couldn't find a date.

Why did the tomato blush?
Because it saw the salad dressing.

Why is a Brussels sprout small and green?
Because if it was big and red, it would be a fire truck.

Why was the stale biscuit so sad?
He was feeling crummy.

What's the difference between boogies and brocolli?
Children don't eat brocolli!

Why couldn't the poppy seed leave the bowling alley?
Because he was on a roll.

Why did the student eat his homework?
The teacher told him it was a piece of cake.

What do you get if you put five ducks in a box?
A box of quackers.

What's a cannibal's favorite takeout?
Pizza with everyone on it.

Why did the man eat at the investment bank?
He loved rich food.

Where do people swap celery with each other?
At the Stalk Exchange.

What did the teddy bear say when he was offered second helpings?
No, thanks. I'm stuffed!

Did you hear about the fruit salad without any pink fruit in it?
It was peachless.

Where do monkeys sleep?
In ape-ricots.

Which musical instrument goes really well with cheese?
The pickle-o.

What has lots of ears, but can't hear anything at all?
A cornfield.

❖

What's green and sings in the vegetable patch?
Elvis Parsley.

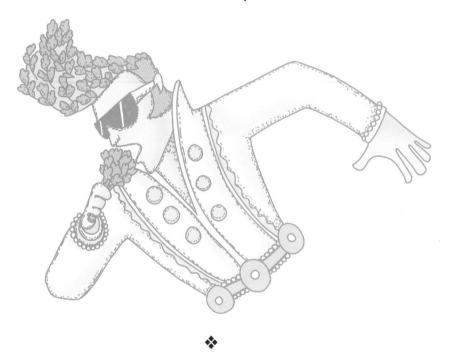

❖

How do you make an apple puff?
Chase it around the kitchen.

❖

Why did the chef serve frozen steak?
He wanted it to melt in your mouth.

What did the flamenco-dancing farmer say to his chickens?
"Oh, lay!"

❖

Where do fish keep their savings?
In riverbanks.

❖

What's round, red, and speaks with a croaky voice?
A hoarse radish.

❖

Which vegetables do elephants like to prepare for dinner?
Squash.

❖

What's round, shiny, and says, "Ahem"?
A cough drop.

❖

Who solved the dessert mystery?
Sherbert Holmes.

When is an Irish potato not an Irish potato?
When it's a French Fry.

Did you hear about the chocolate-covered train?
It was a cocoa-motive.

What did the classical musician love to eat?
Organ-ic chocolate.

What do you get if you whisk butter, sugar, and
eggs together for 37 minutes exactly?
A sore arm.

How do you make hot chocolate?
Leave it out in the sun.

What's the best thing to put in a chocolate bar?
Your teeth.

What wobbles as it flies?
A jellycopter.

Did you hear about the elf who ate too fast?
He was goblin his food.

❖

How do you fix a broken vegetable?
With tomato paste.

❖

When's the best time of day to eat a crisp apple?
Crunchtime.

❖

How do you make a soup golden?
Add 24 carats.

What did the boy say after eating a giant tower-shaped sundae in Paris?
"Eiffel terrible."

What do you give to a sick lemon?
Lemon aid.

Why should you never tell secrets in a farm?
Because the potatoes have eyes and the corn has ears.

❖

Why did the cream squeal?
Someone was whipping it.

What do elves make sandwiches with?
Shortbread.

Why was the undercover agent fired from
his job at the greasy spoon café?
He kept spilling the beans.

What noise does a nut make when it sneezes?
"Cashew!"

What kind of room can you eat?
A mushroom.

Which fruit never ever gets lonely?
A pear.

What did the Hungarian ghost eat for dinner?
Ghoulash.

Why did the bacon laugh?
Because the egg cracked a yolk.

Knock knock.

Figs.

Figs who?

Figs the doorbell—it's pouring out here!

Why did the boy put candy under his pillow?

He wanted sweet dreams.

THE LAUGHTER LIBRARY

Too Much Food For Dinner
by Ed Anuff

Cooking French Food
by Sue Flay

Too Many Beans
by Wynn D. Bottom

Grub's Up
by Carmen Gettit

What the Diner Found Next to His Plate
by Roland Butter

MONSTER MADNESS

Did you hear about the dyslexic demon?
He sold his soul to Santa.

Where do ghosts live?
At the dead end.

Did you hear about the man that used to be a werewolf?
He's all right now-wow-woooooooooo!

How did the boy know what the ghost was getting for Christmas?
He felt his presents.

What does the headless horseman ride?
A night mare.

How do you make a witch itch?
Take away the "w"!

Did you hear about the incredibly brainy monster?
He was called Frank Einstein.

What did the Loch Ness Monster say to the salmon?
"Long time, no sea."

What do you call a dinosaur that never gives up?
Try-try-try-ceratops.

❖

What type of spells did the spinning witch cast?
Dizzy spells.

How can you tell when there's a giant monster under your bed?
When your nose touches the ceiling.

What do you call a nervous witch?
A twitch.

What do you call a skeleton who doesn't feel like getting out of bed?
Lazy bones.

What do you do with a blue monster?
Try to cheer it up.

Why don't witches get sunburns?
They use suntan potion.

❖

Did you hear about the overweight witch?
She went to Weight Witches.

❖

Did you hear about the witch's breakfast cereal?
It went snap, cackle, and pop.

❖

What do trainee witches do at school?
Spelling tests.

❖

How do you describe a smelly witch with loads
of gold stashed away in her cauldron?
Stinking witch.

❖

Why couldn't the frightened archer hit the target?
Because his arrows were all in a quiver.

83

What is a witch's favorite fruit?
Wartermelon.

What happened at the cannibals' wedding?
They toasted the bride and groom.

What's the spookiest candy in the world?
Marshmalloween.

Who lights up a haunted house?
The lights witch.

Why couldn't the ghost order a vodka at the bar?
They didn't serve spirits.

Who cleans a haunted school?
A scaretaker.

Why should witches never lose their tempers
while they're zooming around on a broomstick?
They would fly off the handle.

Did you hear about the witch's enormous mixing pot?
It was called Ron.

Where do you find giant snails?
At the end of giants' fingers.

What do you call a dinosaur wearing a blindfold?
Doyouthinkhesaurus.

What does a wet-weather witch do?
She forecasts rainy spells.

Why didn't the witch wear a flat cap?
There was no point.

What's the scariest player on a soccer team?
The ghoulie.

I have a large, hooked nose, three eyes, and cabbages for ears.
What am I?
Really ugly.

What do cannibals eat on toast?
Baked beings.

❖

What do you do with a green monster?
Wait until it's ripe.

❖

What do you feed an invisible cat?
Evaporated milk.

❖

What do you get when dinosaurs crash their cars?
Tyrannosaurus wrecks.

❖

What happened when Dracula swallowed a sheep?
He felt baaaaaaaaaaaaaad.

❖

What happened when the ghosts went on strike?
A skeleton staff took over.

Where do ghosts swim?
In the Dead Sea.

❖

Why are ghosts dreadful liars?
You can always see through them.

❖

Why are graveyards never deserted?
There's always somebody there.

❖

Why couldn't the skeleton go to the disco?
He had no body to dance with.

❖

Why do demons and ghouls get along so well?
Because demons are a ghoul's best friend.

❖

Where do stinky witches get washed?
In a hubble bubble bath.

❖

What is wicked on the inside and green and knobbly on the outside?
A witch dressed as an avocado.

What type of coffee does a vampire drink?
De-coffin-ated.

What goes "WOO-HA-HA" THUMP?
A monster laughing his head off.

What's the best way to speak to a scary monster?
Long-distance.

Why do dragons sleep during the day?
So they can fight knights.

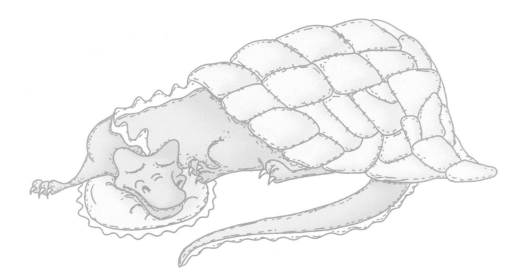

What's Dracula's favorite soup?
Scream of mushroom.

What sport do vampires play?
Batminton.

How do witches make their own hair stand on end?
With scarespray.

What do you get when a dinosaur sneezes?
Out of the way!

What did the mummy order from the diner?
A wrap.

How does a monster count to 17?
On his fingers!

Where do ghouls go swimming?
Lake Eerie.

How do you tell if a monster has a glass eye?
It will come out in the conversation.

How do ghosts send letters overseas?
By scaremail.

How do ghosts begin business letters?
"Tomb it may concern…"

What's a ghost's favorite party game?
Musical scares.

What do you call a vampire that lives in the kitchen drawer?
Count Spatula.

Did you hear about the horribly hungry monster
who ate a sofa and two armchairs?
He had a three-piece-suite tooth.

❖

Which monster is green and gloomy?
The Incredible Sulk.

❖

What does the Abominable Snowman like to cook?
Spag-yeti.

❖

Did you hear about the banshee who wanted to be an actress?
She did a scream test.

❖

How does Frankenstein predict the future?
With a horror-scope.

❖

Why was the ghost so hilarious?
He knocked the audience dead.

❖

What has handles and flies?
A witch in her cauldron.

How do ghouls make their fortunes?
They buy and sell scares on the Shock Exchange.

❖

What is Count Dracula's favorite fruit?
The necktarine.

❖

Which monster can't help picking his nose?
The bogeyman.

❖

How do skeletons keep in touch?
They talk on their bones.

What kind of dog does a vampire own?
A bloodhound.

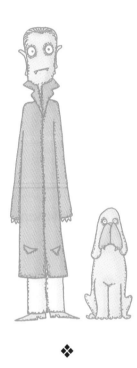

Why did the car stop when it saw the headless monster?
It had a nervous breakdown.

What's the most terrifying ride at the carnival?
The rollerghoster.

What do ghosts and ghouls say to each other at sunset?
Good moaning!

Which monster is the best dancer?
The boogieman.

❖

What do vampires do at eleven o'clock every night?
They have a coffin break.

❖

What do you call a chicken that goes bump in the night?
A poultrygeist.

❖

Did you hear about the lazy skeleton?
He was bone idle.

❖

Why did the two-headed monster ask for more money at the circus?
He claimed that he had an extra mouth to feed.

❖

Why don't skeletons play music in churches?
They have no organs.

What do you call an unidentified wizard on a broomstick?
A flying sorcerer.

What did the archaeologist shout when he opened the tomb?
"Mummy!"

What happened when the two ghosts bumped into
each other in the dark alley?
It was love at first fright.

What do really ugly monsters buy at the local shop?
Grosseries.

Who won the monsters' beauty contest?
No one.

What type of ballroom dancing does a vampire do best?
The fango.

What's a monster's favorite party game?
Swallow the leader.

What will a vampire never order in a restaurant?
Steak.

What has a pointy hat, a broomstick, and a blue face?
A witch holding her breath.

What type of music do demons listen to?
Soul music.

What do birds play at Halloween?
Trick or tweeting.

THE LAUGHTER LIBRARY

The Ghostspotters' Guide
by R. U. A. Spook

They're Devilishly Handsome
by D. Munns

How to Scare
Yourself Silly
by Herr Raising-Pranks

The Indecisive Vampire
by Woody Bite

MEDICAL MISCHIEF

Doctor, doctor, how can I cure flat feet?
With a foot pump.

Doctor, doctor, my nose is running.
No, I think you'll find it's snot.

Doctor, doctor, I feel like a dog!
Sit!

Doctor, doctor, I feel like a set of playing cards.
I'll deal with you later.

Doctor, doctor, I feel like a pair of curtains.
Well, pull yourself together, then.

What did one tonsil say to the other?
"Get dressed—the doctor is taking us out."

Doctor, doctor, can you get rid of my blemishes?
I never make rash promises.

Doctor, doctor, people keep ignoring me.
Next!

Doctor, doctor, can you give me something for my liver?
How about some nice fried onions?

Doctor, doctor, I keep seeing an insect doing pirouettes.
Oh, that's just a bug that's going around.

Doctor, doctor, I think I'm a clock!
Don't get wound up about it.

Doctor, doctor, I feel like a witch's hat.
I see your point.

Doctor, doctor, I'd like a second opinion.
Fine—come back tomorrow.

❖

Doctor, doctor, I think I'm a rubber band!
Stretch yourself out on the couch then.

Doctor, doctor, I have a fish bone stuck in my throat!

Are you choking?

No, I'm serious!

Doctor, doctor, I haven't slept for days!

Why not?

Because I sleep at night!

Doctor, doctor, I keep getting sharp stabbing
pains in my eye when I drink tea!

Then take the spoon out of the cup.

Doctor, doctor, I keep seeing double.

Take a seat, please.

Which one?

Doctor, doctor, I keep thinking I'm a bridge.

What's come over you?

Six cars, three trucks, and a bus.

Doctor, doctor, I keep thinking I'm a goat.

How long has this been going on for?

Since I was a kid.

Doctor, doctor, I keep thinking I'm a bell.
Take these pills. If they don't work, give me a ring.

❖

Doctor, doctor, what can you give me for wind?
Here's a kite.

❖

Doctor, doctor, I think I'm a leech.
Get out of here, sucker!

❖

How do dentists prepare for an earthquake?
They brace themselves.

❖

Doctor, doctor, can you help me out?
**Certainly, put your arm through mine and I'll escort
you off the premises.**

❖

Doctor, doctor, I can't stop stealing things!
**Take these pills. If they don't work, get me a plasma TV
and a bag of gold.**

Doctor, doctor, I think I'm a frog.
Hop up onto this stool for a checkup.

❖

Doctor, doctor, I only have 59 seconds to live!
I'll see you in a minute.

❖

Doctor, doctor, I'm terrified of squirrels!
You must be nuts.

❖

Doctor, doctor, I've just swallowed a clock!
Don't panic, there's no cause for alarm.

Doctor, doctor, I think I need glasses.
I think you do. This is a deli.

❖

Doctor, doctor, I feel like a bee.
Buzz off!

❖

Doctor, doctor, I feel like a spoon.
Sit down and don't stir!

❖

Why did the boy creep past the medical cabinet?
He didn't want to disturb the sleeping pills.

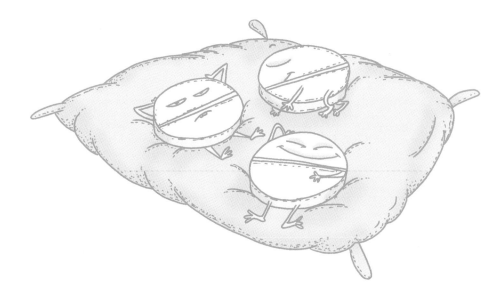

Doctor, doctor, do you have anything for a terrible headache?
Yes, bash yourself twice on the head with this mallet.

❖

Doctor, doctor, I feel like a pack of lunch meat.
That's a lot of baloney.

❖

Doctor, doctor, I'm becoming invisible.
Yes, I can see that you're not all there.

❖

Doctor, doctor, I keep thinking I'm a caterpillar.
You'll soon change.

❖

Doctor, doctor, I can't get to sleep at night.
Sit right on the edge of the bed and you'll soon drop off.

❖

Doctor, doctor, I keep thinking I'm a desk.
You're just letting things get on top of you.

Doctor, doctor, I keep thinking I'm a calculator.
Great, you can help me with my accounts then.

Doctor, doctor, I smell like fish.
You poor sole.

Doctor, doctor, I can't help frightening people.
Argggggghhhhhhh!

Doctor, doctor, I have a big, juicy strawberry on my head.
I'll give you some cream for that.

Doctor, doctor, when I poke my finger here, it hurts.
And here… and here! What's wrong with me?
Your finger's broken!

Doctor, doctor, I think I'm suffering from a bad case of déjà vu.
I've seen you before.

Doctor, doctor, will I be able to play the recorder after the operation?

Yes, of course.

Excellent! I've never been able to play it before!

Doctor, doctor, I'm a compulsive thief!

You'd better take something for that.

Doctor, doctor, I've swallowed my pen!

Don't worry, you can borrow mine.

❖

Doctor, doctor, I keep thinking I'm a wigwam and then a teepee.

Hmmm. You're definitely two tents.

Doctor, doctor, I keep thinking I'm a plant.
We must get to the root of this problem.

❖

Which ghosts haunt hospital wards?
Surgical spirits.

❖

Doctor, doctor, I've swallowed a roll of film!
Let's hope nothing serious develops.

❖

Doctor, doctor, how can I stop my nose from running?
Trip it up.

Doctor, doctor, I keep thinking I'm a boa constrictor.
You can't get around me, you know.

❖

Doctor, doctor, my snoring's keeping me awake.
Well, sleep in another room!

❖

How did the patient get to the doctor so quickly?
He flu.

❖

What did one eye say to the other eye?
Between you and me, something smells.

❖

Doctor, doctor, I think I've got woodworm.
How boring for you!

❖

What do you call someone who sits in a doctor's waiting
room for hours and hours?
Patient.

❖

Doctor, doctor, I think I'm a strawberry.
Hmmm… You're in a jam.

Why are false teeth like stars?
They come out at night.

How do dentists check crocodiles' teeth?
Very carefully.

What did the tiger eat after he'd had all his teeth pulled out?
The dentist.

Where do dentists go sailing?
Up root canals.

What did the dentist say when the patient told him
a terrible joke about his sweet tooth?
"That's rotten."

Nurse, how is the little boy who swallowed the coins?
No change yet.

Why did the queen go to the dentist?
To get her teeth crowned.

What type of fish carries out operations?
A sturgeon.

When is it time to see the dentist?
Tooth-hurty.

What did the dentist say when she stood up in front of the judge?
"I swear to tell the tooth, the whole tooth, and nothing but the tooth."

If you broke your leg in two places, what would you do?
Never go back to those two places!

What's the most musical bone?
The trom-bone.

What do you call a couple of doctors?
A pair-a-medics.

THE LAUGHTER LIBRARY

The Man Who
Bumped His Head
by I. C. Stars

When Teeth Go Bad
by D. Kaye

The Dodgy Diagnosis
by Shirley U. Jeste

Bites and Rashes
by Ivan Itch

How to Look Surprised
by Fay Slift

The Patient with the
Exploding Bottom
by Stan Wellback

The Doctor Who Couldn't
Stop Complaining
by Mona Lott

Under the Magnifying Glass
by Mike Robes

SCHOOL SHOCKERS

Why was the school cook arrested?
Because she beat the eggs and whipped the cream.

❖

Why did the boy take a ladder to school?
He had heard it was a high school.

❖

How did the Vikings send secret messages during lessons?
By Norse Code.

❖

What do elves do after school?
Gnomework.

❖

What did the set square say to the protractor?
Take me to your ruler.

❖

How do you fix a broken tuba?
With a tubaglue.

What was the dog awarded when he left college?
A pedigree.

What did the computer eat for dinner?
A byte.

Well, son, what did you learn at your first day of school?
Not enough—we have to go back tomorrow.

❖

Why do learner witches need dictionaries?
They can't spell.

If two's company and three's a crowd, then what are four and five?

Nine.

❖

Why was Queen Elizabeth I buried at Westminster Abbey?

Because she was dead.

❖

What did the 0 say to the 8?

"Cool belt."

❖

Which snake is good at arithmetic?

An adder.

What runs but never walks, has a mouth but never talks,
and has a bed but never sleeps?
A river.

❖

If the red house was made of red bricks and the brown house was made
of brown bricks, what was the green house made of?
Glass.

❖

Which is fastest, cold or heat?
Heat. You can catch a cold.

❖

Did you hear about the cannibal that was expelled from school?
He was buttering up the teachers.

❖

If I slice three pears into five pieces, what do I have?
Really sticky fingers.

❖

Is it easier to write with your right hand or your left hand?
Neither. It's easier to write with a pen.

What did the enormous computer eat for dinner?
A megabyte!

What do computer teachers pack as a snack?
Chips.

What do really tiny computer teachers pack as a snack?
Microchips.

What do you call a Roman emperor with a cold?
Julius Sneezer.

What do you get if you cross a vampire and a teacher?
Blood tests.

What kind of lighting did Noah use for his ark?
Floodlights.

What is an insect's best subject at school?
Mothematics.

What did Henry VIII become on his 21st birthday?
A year older.

What foreign language are birds really good at?
Portugeese.

What did the teacher say to the naughty egg?
"You're eggspelled."

What kind of meals do geometry teachers enjoy?
Square meals.

What's the fruitiest lesson at school?
History. It's full of dates.

What's the longest sentence ever?
Life imprisonment.

What's the longest word in the world?
**"Smiles," because there's a mile between
the first letter and the last.**

Where do bad spellers look up words?
In a dickshunerry.

Where was the Magna Carta signed?
At the bottom.

Which tree has square roots?
A geometry.

What are you going to be when you leave school?
Older.

Where did the surfer learn all his stuff?
At boarding school.

Why did the girl go to night school?
Because she wanted to learn to read in the dark.

Why did the magician's son do so well at school?
He wasn't afraid of trick questions.

Why did the teacher wear sunglasses?
Because his class was so bright.

Why did the girl keep her guitar in the fridge?
Because she liked cool music.

Why did the girl stare at the orange juice carton?
Because it said "concentrate" on the label.

Why did the Romans build straight roads?
So they didn't go around the bend.

❖

Where do ghosts do their homework?
In an exorcise book.

❖

Why is Europe like a dirty frying pan?
Because it has Greece at the bottom.

❖

Why is six scared of seven?
Because seven ate nine.

❖

What comes before 11?
Our letters, if we're lucky.

❖

Why don't cannibals like the equation four plus four?
Because they get eight.

What's purple and burns?
The Grape Fire of London.

Why was the computer coughing and sneezing and sniffing?
Because it had a virus.

Did you hear about the schoolboy who was asked to use the word
"fascinate" in a sentence?
**He said, "I have ten buttons on my cardigan,
but I can only fasten eight!"**

Why was the cross-eyed teacher's class rioting?
She couldn't control her pupils.

Why did the pupil think the teacher had a crush on him?
She put Xs all over his homework.

❖

Which animal is the best with numbers?
Rabbits. They can multiply really quickly.

❖

Where did Noah keep his oldest bees?
In the ark hive.

❖

What was the dentist's favorite subject at school?
Flossophy.

❖

Why was the math textbook miserable?
It had too many problems.

❖

Why was the school girl excited?
Because the teacher had told her to wait there for the present.

Why didn't the girl go to the end of the school dinner line?
There was already somebody there.

Where was Queen Elizabeth II crowned?
On her head.

Where did Christopher Columbus land
when he arrived in the Americas?
On his feet.

Did you hear about the chick that misbehaved in all its classes?
It was eggspelled!

Who invented fractions?
Henry the Eighth.

Why was Rome built at night?
Because it wasn't built in a day.

Why was the music teacher locked out of his classroom?
The keys were on the piano.

Which tools come in handy during a math lesson?
Multi-pliers.

What do we do with crude oil?
Teach it good manners.

❖

Why was the multiplication worksheet sad?
It had too many problems.

Why was the broom late for school?

It overswept.

Why did the astronomer jump into the boxing ring?

He wanted to see stars.

What was Camelot famous for?

Its knight life.

❖

If you cut a potato into sixteenths, what will you have?

Chips.

What's the capital of Peru?
P.

❖

Who invented King Arthur's round table?
Sir Cumference.

❖

Which month has 28 days?
All of them.

❖

What is adding?
It's the noise a doorbell makes.

❖

Why did the teacher put the lights on?
Because the class was dim.

❖

What did the geometry teacher order for dessert?
Pi.

Why did Henry VIII have so many wives?
He liked to chop around.

❖

What do elves learn at school?
The elf-abet.

❖

Which word is always spelled incorrectly?
Incorrectly.

❖

How do pupils get straight As?
By using a ruler.

❖

Why did one pencil tell the other pencil
that it looked old and worn out?
Because it was blunt.

❖

Which are the coldest sort of triangles?
Ice-soceles.

❖

How do bees get to school?
On the buzz.

Why did the teacher jump into the swimming pool?
She wanted to test the water.

What's the fastest way to double your money?
Fold it in half.

Where does success come before work?
In a dictionary.

What is a polygon?
A dead parrot.

Which school days start with the letter T?
Today and tomorrow.

What is a cow's favorite lesson?
Moo-sic.

Have you heard the joke about the blunt pencil?
Sorry, there's no point.

Which schoolbag is always tired?
A knapsack.

THE LAUGHTER LIBRARY

The Enormous Sum
by Adam Upp

Top of the Class
by Jeanie Yuss

I Nearly Missed the School Bus
by Justin Thyme

The Eager Pupil
by I. Wanda Know

SEASIDE SILLINESS

How many tickles does it take to make an octopus laugh?
Tentacles

How did pirates sleep on galleons?
With their eyes shut.

There are two goldfish in a tank. What does one goldfish say to the other goldfish?
"Do you know how to drive this thing?"

What did the sea say to the dolphin?
Nothing, it just waved.

What do you call a fish with no eyes?
Fsh.

What do you call a fish with four eyes?
Fiiiish.

What do you call a pirate with a wooden leg, a very pointy hook, and a parrot stuck in each ear?
Anything you like, he can't hear you!

How much did the pirate pay for his wooden leg and terrifyingly sharp hook?
An arm and a leg.

What do you give a deaf fish?
A herring aid.

How do cod and mackerel watch the news?
On a telefishon.

How did the tiny shellfish cross the seabed?
By taxi crab.

Why did the cottage go on a diet?
It wanted to be a lighthouse.

What lives under the sea and carries lots of people to and fro?
An octo-bus.

❖

What's black, incredibly rude, and floats on water?
Crude oil.

Where can you find an ocean with no water?
On a map.

Why do fish avoid computers?
They don't want to get caught in the internet.

Why are pirates called pirates?
Because they ARRRRRR!

Why couldn't the pirate play cards?
Because he was sitting on the deck.

Why did the animal cruelty officer close down
the seafood restaurant?
They were battering the fish.

Why did the crab blush?
Because the seaweed.

What do you find in the middle of the ocean?
The letter "e."

Why did the sailor carry a piece of rope onto the boat?
Because he was the skipper.

❖

What's a pirate's favorite boxing punch?
The right hook.

❖

What's a pirate's favorite fairy tale?
Booty and the Beast.

❖

What's a pirate's favorite letter of the alphabet?
R.

❖

Why did the pirate's phone go, "beeeep … beeeep … beeeep"?
He left it off the hook.

❖

Why didn't the sea captain's radio work in rough seas?
It was on the wrong wavelength.

❖

What do you get if you cross a snowman and a shark?
Frostbite.

What's the best way to get in touch with a fish?
Drop it a line.

Why are fish easy to weigh?
They have their own scales.

What's the difference between a fish and a piano?
You can't tuna fish.

Which is the most precious fish in the world?
A goldfish.

What did the jazz musician eat for his fish supper?
He had sole.

What did the blue whale say when he collided
with the bottlenose dolphin?
"I didn't do it on porpoise."

What type of lettuce did they serve on the Titanic?
Iceberg.

What are the strongest creatures in the ocean?
Mussels.

Where do very young fish go every morning?
Plaice school.

❖

How did the magician cut the sea in half?
With a sea saw.

❖

What barks, has flippers, eats fish, and lives in Washington?
The presidential seal.

❖

Which is the saddest creature in the sea?
The blue whale.

❖

What is a fish's favorite party game?
Tide-and-seek.

❖

Which seabird can dance?
A pelican-can.

❖

Why do fish swim in salt water?
Because pepper would make them sneeze.

Why are some fish stuck at the bottom of the ocean?
Because they dropped out of school.

❖

What does an octopus wear in the winter?
A coat of arms.

❖

What did the magician say to the fisherman?
"Pick a cod, any cod."

❖

Who was the first underwater spy?
James Pond.

What happens when you throw a purple rock into the Red Sea?
It gets wet.

❖

What's green and knobbly and spends a lot of time under the sea?
An avocado wearing scuba gear.

❖

Where does seaweed look for a job?
In the "Kelp Wanted" section of the newspaper.

❖

What's the best way to catch a fish?
Get someone to throw it at you.

❖

Which is the shiniest fish in the sea?
The starfish.

❖

How did the ship's carpenter break all of his teeth?
By chewing his nails.

❖

What's the fastest thing in the sea?
A motor-pike.

Why are dolphins brighter than humans?
**They can train a human to stand at the side of a pool
and throw fish to them.**

❖

What's a carpenter's favorite sea creature?
A hammerhead shark.

❖

What do you get if you cross a fish with an elephant?
Swimming trunks.

❖

Who do fish borrow money from?
A loan shark.

❖

What do you find on very small beaches?
Microwaves.

❖

Why are seagulls called seagulls?
Because if they flew over bays, they would be bagels.

❖

Who dresses like a cowboy and lives in the ocean?
Billy the Squid.

Where did the ship go when it was unwell?
It visited the docks.

Why was the pupil's school report wet?
Because her grades were all below C level.

Who lives in a sandcastle?
A sandwitch.

❖

How does a pod of dolphins make its mind up?
They flipper coin.

What does a groom wear to an underwater wedding?
A very wet suit.

Why don't you ever see penguins near the UK?
They're scared of Wales.

Why can't penguins fly?
They can't afford plane tickets.

Why can't penguins fly?
They can't afford plane tickets.

What do penguins have for lunch?
Icebergers.

Which sea creatures are the biggest cry babies?
Whales.

Why wasn't the girl scared when a shark swam past her?
It was a man-eating shark.

What do you call a man-eating cod?
Fish-ious.

What's the coldest creature in the sea?
A blue whale.

What did the seaweed say when it was stuck to
the bottom of the speedboat?
"Kelp!!!!!"

What is a pirate's favorite school subject?
Arrrrrrrt.

What should you wear on your feet at the seaside?
Sand-als.

Why did the fish take such a long time to make up his mind?
He wanted to mullet over.

What are qualified divers presented with?
A deep-loma.

What kind of hairstyle does the sea have?
Wavy.

THE LAUGHTER LIBRARY

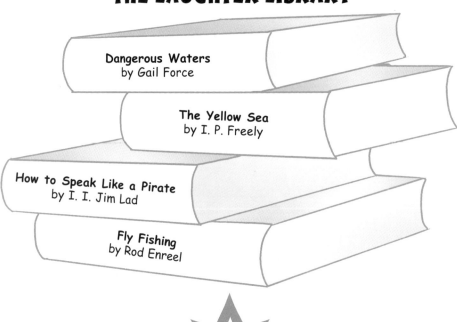

Dangerous Waters
by Gail Force

The Yellow Sea
by I. P. Freely

How to Speak Like a Pirate
by I. I. Jim Lad

Fly Fishing
by Rod Enreel

COSMIC CAPERS

How do you get a baby astronaut to go to sleep?
Rocket.

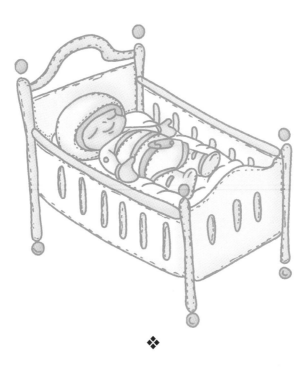

Did you hear about the cashew who went into orbit?
He was an astronut.

What did one asteroid say to the other asteroid?
"Pleased to meteor."

❖

What's ET short for?
Because he has little legs.

Why don't astronauts take eggs into space?
Because eggs're terrestrial!

❖

When do astronauts eat?
At launch time.

❖

Which is the most precious planet?
Saturn. It has a lot of rings.

❖

What do you put on a space horse?
A saddle-lite.

❖

What do young astronauts sit on during take-off?
Booster seats.

❖

How does the Solar System hold up its pants?
With an asteroid belt.

If meteorites collide with planets, what do you
call meteorites that miss?
Meteowrongs.

❖

What do aliens cook their breakfast on?
An unidentified frying object.

❖

How did the alien tie his shoelaces?
With an astroknot.

❖

Why was the thirsty astronaut loitering near the computer keyboard?
He was looking for the space bar.

❖

What do you call a spaceship with a faulty thermostat?
A frying saucer.

❖

Did you hear about the man who was whisked
away by alien teddy bears?
He had a close encounter of the furred kind.

Why don't aliens celebrate each other's birthdays?
They don't like to give away their presents.

Where do aliens leave their spaceships?
At parking meteors.

What's the most important thing to do if you're
going to have a party in space?
Plan-et.

How do you know when the moon isn't hungry?
When it's full.

What type of songs do planets love to hear?
Nep-tunes.

What do astronauts do when they get dirty?
They take a meteor shower.

How do you know if the spaceship's engine is running?
When you have to run after it!

Why didn't the Sun go to college?
Because it already had a million degrees.

What holds the moon up?
Moon beams.

What type of crazy insect lives on the moon?
A lunar-tick.

❖

What kind of poems do you find in outer space?
Uni-verse.

❖

How does the man-in-the-moon cut his hair?
Eclipse it!

❖

What type of astronaut can jump higher than a house?
All of them—houses can't jump.

❖

Did you hear about the supersonic egg?
It couldn't be beaten.

What's the center of gravity?
The letter V.

What sort of turf do aliens play football on?
Astroturf.

Did you hear the one about the spaceship from the far-off galaxy?
It was out of this world.

What did the boy star say to the girl star?
"Do you want to glow out with me?"

Where do aliens go to build sandcastles?
The galax-seashore.

Which star is the most dangerous?
The shooting star.

What's a light-year?
Same as a normal year, but with less fat.

What did the alien say to the pump at the gas station?
**"It's very rude to stick your finger in your ear when
I'm talking to you!"**

Why don't astronauts get hungry until they've
been in space for a few hours?
They've just had a big launch.

Which star wears dark glasses?
A film star.

Why don't astronauts keep their jobs for long?
Because after their training, they're always fired.

❖

Why didn't the Apollo astronauts stay on the moon?
Because it was full.

❖

Which astronaut wears the biggest space helmet?
The one with the biggest head.

❖

Did you hear about the alien with perfect eyesight?
He had 20-20-20 vision.

What do you get if you cross Earth's atmosphere and a hot drink?
Gravi-tea.

How did the aliens hurt the farmer?
They landed on his corn.

Where do little green men get their eggs?
From the little green hen.

What do aliens rest their teacups on?
Flying saucers.

What did Venus say to Saturn?
"Why not give me a ring sometime?"

❖

What's big, bright, round, and very, very silly?
A fool moon.

❖

What should a car driver do if he sees a space man?
Park in it, man.

❖

What was the alien's bag full of on Halloween?
A Martian-mallow.

Why did the girl become an astronaut?
Because she was no earthly good.

What do you call an overweight alien?
An extra-cholesterol.

How does the barber cut the man in the moon's hair?
E-clipse it.

Where do martians go to drink?
A Mars Bar.

What's the easiest way to experience time travel?
Throw your clock at the wall.

❖

Where do you find black holes?
In black socks.

Why are parties on the moon always so dull?
There's no atmosphere.

What did the alien Santa say when he visited Earth?
UFO-O-O.

What does the man in the moon use instead of plates?
Satellite dishes.

How do astronomers know that the universe isn't heavy?
Because distances are measured in light years.

Why did the astrophysicist fit a knocker on his front door?
He wanted to win the No Bell Prize.

Why did the alien spacecraft land
outside the bedroom door?
The landing light was on.

What did the alien say to the plant?
"Take me to your weeder."

What happened when the astrophysicist
slammed his front door?
There was a Big Bang.

How many astronomers
does it take to change a lightbulb?
None. They prefer the dark.

THE LAUGHTER LIBRARY

Measuring Really Big Planets
by Sir Cumference

Famous Space Robots
by Anne Droid

Sudden Darkness
by E. Clipz

DIY Space Travel
by Bill Jerome Rocket

In the Meteor's Path
by Luke Out

Fly Me to the Moon
by Tay Cough

The Masked Alien
by Hugh R. Ewe

The UFO Mysteries
by N. Igma

What the Astronaut Found on the Sparkly Planet
by Chris Tall

Bringing the Universe into View
by Telly Scope

The Unemployed Astronaut
by Anita Job

Digital Displays Are Bad and Wrong
by Anna Logg

The Aliens' Guide to Table Manners
by Megan A. Mess

I Saw An Alien
by Omar Goodness

SILLY SPORTS

What do you call a pig that does karate?
A pork chop.

Why wouldn't the soccer player cross the road?
It was offside.

How do high-speed witches travel?
By vroomstick.

Did you hear about the racecar with the wooden engine?
It wooden go.

What's striped, furry, and goes "meeeeeowwwwwww"?
A cat in a racecar.

❖

Why is it sweltering hot after a tennis match?
All the fans have gone home.

❖

Did you hear about the sports equipment
manufacturer with his stereo on full blast?
He was making a racket.

❖

What did Robin Hood say when he was
almost hit at the archery tournament?
"That was an arrow escape!"

❖

Which part of a sports stadium never stays the same?
The changing rooms.

What should a football team do if the stadium is flooded?
Bring on their subs.

❖

Why was Cinderella a terrible tennis player?
She kept running away from the ball.

❖

What do martial artists suffer from in the winter?
Kung-flu.

❖

What did the boy say when his dad told him not to
swim on an empty stomach?
"OK, I'll swim on my back."

❖

What is harder to catch the faster you run?
Your breath.

Why wouldn't the skeleton bungee jump into the Grand Canyon?
He had no guts.

What's the fastest milk in the world?
Full-fat milk. It's pasteurized before you know it.

What's the fastest vegetable on earth?
A runner bean.

❖

Why are goalies stinking rich?
Because they are good savers.

What's green and runs around the garden?
A hedge.

Did you hear about the scarecrow who won a gold medal?
He was out standing in his field.

Which animal is always found at baseball games?
A bat.

Why was Cinderella a terrible soccer player?
Because her coach was a pumpkin.

Which way does a chicken swim around a pool?
Cluck-wise.

What did the golfer eat for lunch?
A sand wedge.

If marathon runners suffer from athlete's foot,
what do soldiers suffer from?
Missile toe.

What did the parachuting insect shout as it jumped
out of the airplane?
"Earwig go!"

Why did the champion racehorse lose the big race?
It had hay fever.

How did the soccer field turn into a right-angled triangle?
Somebody took a corner.

What do babies and basketball players have in common?
They're both really good at dribbling.

Where do football players go dancing?
At a football.

Which letter is most popular with golfers?
Tee.

Which insect was terrible in goal?
The fumblebee.

What is a marathon runner's favorite subject?
Jography.

Who can spot promising players and tie seventeen
different types of knot?
A scout.

Why should bowling alleys be kept quiet?
So you can hear a pin drop.

Why did the basketball players spin the ball on their fingertips?
Because it was the Whirled Cup.

Why did the football player kick the ball around his own back yard?
It was a home game.

What's a horse's favorite sport?
Stable tennis.

What kind of cats are great at bowling?

Alley cats.

❖

Why should people never fall in love with tennis players?

Because to them, love means nothing.

❖

Do undersea creatures play football?

Yes, they do. There are 20,000 Leagues Under the Sea.

❖

Why is it easy to forecast the weather on days when games are scheduled?

There are always showers after the final whistle.

Why did the ambulance arrive at the soccer game
after 90 minutes were up?
The players were into injury time.

❖

Why was the pirate such an amazing boxer?
Because of his left hook.

❖

Why do penguins do so well in car races?
Because they are always in Pole position.

❖

Why don't you ever go rock climbing?
I would if I were a little boulder.

❖

Why did they have to stop the basketball game and mop the floor?
Because the players kept dribbling.

Why was the tennis court wet?
Because of the floodlights.

Did you hear about the crowd of potatoes watching the tennis match?
They kept their eyes peeled.

What did the boy's mom say when he wanted money to
buy shoes for gym?
"Tell Jim to buy his own shoes."

What happened when the monkey scored a goal?
The crowd went bananas.

Why didn't the dog do martial arts?
Because it was a boxer.

How do football players stay cool during a match?
Because of the fans.

Doctor, doctor, I have a fear of hurdles.
You'll get over it.

Did you hear about the football player whose
ambition was to be an artist?
He liked to draw.

What happens to joggers who run behind cars?
They get exhausted.

Why is it dangerous to tell jokes while ice skating?
The ice might crack up.

Why did the golfer wear two pairs of trousers?
In case he got a hole in one.

Where do old bowling balls get thrown?
In the gutter.

What's the angriest part of a goal?
The crossbar.

❖

What's the hungriest part of a goal?
The goalmouth.

What do you call a really tiny sports fan?
A speck-tator.

❖

Why are fish so bad at tennis?
Because they hate getting close to the net.

❖

Did you hear about the monk
who longed to be a football player?
He was trying to kick the habit.

❖

Why did the skier cry after he hit a tree?
Because it was a weeping willow.

❖

When does it rain football players?
When it's teaming down.

What did the fishing rod say to the trout?
"Catch you later!"

Why was the computer such a terrific golfer?
It had a hard drive.

How do you start a teddy bear race?
"Ready, teddy, go!"

What goes "putt, putt, putt, putt"?
A very bad golfer.

What did the crowd shout
when the ghost flew into the net?
Ghoul!

❖

Why do basketball players love cookies?
They can dunk them.

❖

What's the best time of year
to bounce on a trampoline?
Springtime!

❖

Why did the runner never forget anything?
He was always jogging his memory.

❖

How do you start a jello race?
Get set!

What do you call a pig that plays basketball?
A ball hog.

What's the fastest cake in the world?
Scone.

How do you know when a referee is having a great time?
He whistles while he works.

Why was Tarzan banned from the golf course?
He screamed with every swing.

THE LAUGHTER LIBRARY

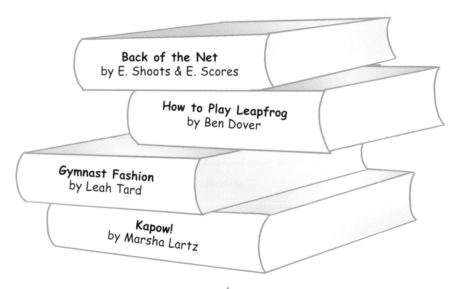

Back of the Net
by E. Shoots & E. Scores

How to Play Leapfrog
by Ben Dover

Gymnast Fashion
by Leah Tard

Kapow!
by Marsha Lartz

GRINS AND GIGGLES

How do trees get on the internet?
They log in.

If two shirt collars had a race, which would win?
Neither—it would end in a tie.

What's green and smells of yellow paint?
Green paint.

❖

What did the Spanish firefighter call his twin sons?
José and Hose B.

Why would you take a mallet to bed with you?
So you could hit the sack.

❖

What type of house weighs the least of all?
A light house.

❖

What did the traffic light say to the car?
"Don't look, I'm changing!"

❖

What do Rupert The Bear and Winnie The Pooh have in common?
They both have the same middle name.

❖

What do you call a boomerang that doesn't come back?
A stick.

❖

What's a lumberjack's favorite month?
Sep-timber

❖

How can you walk through walls?
Open the door.

Where do books go to sleep?
Under their covers.

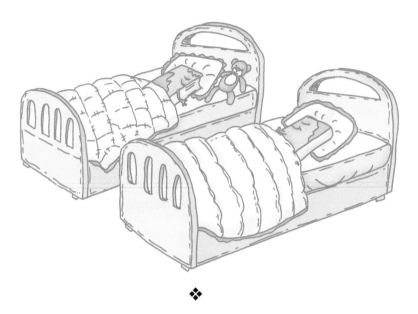

What do you call a man in a red and white outfit
who claps his hands at Christmas?
Santapplause.

What do you call a man with a purply-browny-yellowy
mark on his forehead?
Bruce.

What do you always get on your birthday?
Another year older.

What do you call a pack of wolves?
Wolfgang.

What do you call James Bond when he's taking a bath?
Bubble O Seven.

What goes up, but never comes down?
Your age.

What do you get if you cross a chicken with a cement mixer?
A brick-layer.

What do you get if you cross a painter and
a decorator with a police officer?
A brush with the law.

Why is Santa a good gardener?
Because he likes to hoe, hoe, hoe.

What do you call a lazy young kangaroo?
A pouch potato.

What do you get if you cross a snake with a builder?
A boa constructor.

Why was the dumbbell late?
It got held up at the gym.

What do you get when you cross a skeleton with a detective?
Sherlock Bones.

What has a bottom at the top?
Your legs!

❖

Who sneaks around at Christmas parties?
Mince spies.

❖

Why was the taxi driver fired?
He was driving customers away.

❖

What sits on the seabed and shakes?
A nervous wreck.

❖

Why are Christmas trees like clumsy knitters?
They both drop their needles.

❖

What happens when Father Christmas gets stuck up the chimney?
He gets Santaclaustrophobia.

❖

Why does a milking stool only have three legs?
Because the cow has the udder.

What type of stories does the sea captain tell his children?
Ferry stories.

What wears shoes but has no feet?
The pavement.

Why did the girl take the pencil to bed with her?
She wanted to draw the curtains.

❖

What's a fun night out for a geologist?
A rock concert.

❖

What did the lovestruck stamp say to the envelope?
"I'm stuck on you."

What's brown and sticky?
A stick.

❖

What stays in the corner, but travels all around the world?
A stamp.

What did the girl say when she gave herself a haircut?
"It won't be long now."

❖

What's pink and fluffy?
Pink fluff.

❖

What's blue and fluffy?
Pink fluff holding its breath.

❖

Did you hear about the clothes line robbery?
A pair of shorts was the victim of a hold up.

What did the carrot stick say to the home-baked crisp?
"Want to go for a dip?"

❖

Did you hear about the actor who fell through the floor?
It was just a stage he was going through.

❖

Where did the Pilgrims land when they came to America?
On their feet.

❖

Who pulls Santa's sleigh when the weather is wet?
Raindeer.

What's the difference between a well-dressed
gentleman and an exhausted dog?
One wears an expensive suit and the other just pants.

❖

When is a car not a car?
When it turns into a garage.

❖

Where can you always find diamonds?
In your playing cards.

❖

Someone said that you sounded like an owl.
Who?

❖

What makes a ringing noise when they land on the floor by
Santa's front door?
Jingle Bills.

❖

What's the name of the country where reindeer
run around and around in circles?
Lapland.

What's round and dangerous?
A vicious circle.

What has a long tail, colorful feathers, and wears a bow?
A birthday pheasant.

What's green, has four arms, four legs, two heads,
two trunks, and goes, "Bleurgh!"
Two seasick holidaymakers.

Where did the king keep his armies?
Up his sleevies.

Which part of a mermaid is the heaviest?
The scales.

What did the big candle say to the little candle?
"You're too young to go out."

Why did the newspaper blush?
It saw the comic strip.

❖

Who stole the sponge from the bathroom?
The robber duck.

❖

What sound do porcupines make when they hug?
"Ouch!"

❖

Why did Tarzan buy balloons, fireworks, and crazy hats?
He wanted to have a swinging party.

Why did the man wear a banana skin on each foot?
He wanted a pair of slippers.

What did the sink say to the leaky faucet?
"You're a drip."

Which is the tiredest part of a car?
The exhaust pipe.

Why are elephants all wrinkly?
Have you ever tried to iron one?

What has four wheels and flies?
A garbage truck.

❖

What do you call a judge with no thumbs?
Justice Fingers.

❖

Why are garbage collectors miserable?
Because they're always down in the dumps.

❖

Why did James Bond sleep in?
He was an undercover agent.

❖

What's brown, smelly, and sounds like a bell?
Duuuuung!

❖

Why did the belt go to prison?
Because it held up a pair of pants.

❖

What flavor squash do monsters slurp?
Lemon and slime.

Why is everyone footsore and weary on April 1st?
Because they've just had a long March.

❖

Why are pianos so hard to open?
The keys are inside.

❖

Which flowers grow right under your nose?
Tulips.

❖

What can you always count on?
Your fingers.

❖

A man walks into a bar.
Ouch.

❖

Why was the civil engineer boring?
It was the only way to make a tunnel.

❖

Which part of a turkey has the most rhythm?
The drumsticks.

Why did the girl go to school in a helicopter?
She wanted higher education.

❖

Why did the girl take a scooter to bed?
She didn't want to walk in her sleep.

❖

Why did the toilet paper make a dash down the hill?
It wanted to get to the bottom.

❖

What did Cinderella say when her photos weren't ready on time?
"Some day my prints will come."

Why did the man put his money in the freezer?
He wanted cold, hard cash.

❖

Why didn't the billionaire use soap?
Because he wanted to stay filthy rich.

❖

Why don't people watch TV shows about origami?
Because they're paper view.

❖

Where do cows go to relax?
To the moovies.

Why is a bride like a telephone?
They both have rings.

Why is it expensive to raise a baby?
Because they are dear little things.

Which of Santa's reindeers has the worst temper?
Rude-olph.

What goes up and down but does not move?
Stairs.

Which is the most musical insect?
The humbug.

What is a dentist's favorite musical instrument?
A tuba toothpaste.

Why was the musician so upset?
He couldn't compose himself.

❖

What do snowmen sing at parties?
"Freeze a jolly good fellow…"

❖

What do undercover agents play when they go on a journey?
I spy.

❖

How do you join the brownies?
Rope them all together.

❖

What is full of holes, but can still hold water?
A sponge.

❖

What's the capital of England?
E.

❖

When do long-distance drivers stop for a snack?
When they see a fork in the road.

What did the horse wear at the beach?
Clip clops.

How do you make a bandstand?
Take away their seats.

What never asks a question but always demands an answer?
A telephone.

❖

How do you turn soup into gold?
Add 24 carrots.

Why do rabbits have fur coats?
Because they'd look silly in leather jackets.

How do you get rid of varnish?
Take away the "r"!

What kind of driver never gets a speeding ticket?
A screwdriver.

❖

What do cats put in their drinks?
Mice cubes.

What do the letter A and a rose have in common?
Bs come after them both.

Did you hear about the embarrassed toilet?
It was flushed.

Why were the Middle Ages so dark?
Because there were so many knights.

How can you make your money go a long way?
Put your piggy bank in a rocket.

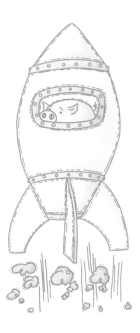

Why did the ghost get into trouble at school?
It spook out of turn.

Do you want to hear a long joke?
Jooooooooooooooooooooooooooooooooooke.

What do you call a fairy that stands in cow dung?
Stinkerbell.

THE LAUGHTER LIBRARY

Navel Gazing
by Belle E. Button

Whodunnit?
by Howard I. Know

The End of the World
by R. McGeddon

My Life as a Lion Tamer
by Claude Bottom

How to Resign
by Ike Witt

Car Maintenance For Idiots
by M. T. Tank

Ooops, My Trousers Fell Down!
by Lucy Lastick

Casual Beach Footwear
by Philippe Fillop